Look Inside Animal Homes
Look Inside a Beaver's Lodge

by Megan Cooley Peterson

Consulting Editor: Gail Saunders-Smith, PhD

Consultant: Marsha A. Sovada
USGS Northern Prairie Wildlife Research Center

CAPSTONE PRESS
a capstone imprint

Pebble Plus is published by Capstone Press,
1710 Roe Crest Drive, North Mankato, Minnesota 56003.
www.capstonepub.com

Books published by Capstone Press are manufactured with paper
containing at least 10 percent post-consumer waste.

Library of Congress Cataloging-in-Publication Data
Peterson, Megan Cooley.
   Look inside a beaver's lodge / by Megan Cooley Peterson.
      p. cm.—(Pebble plus. Look inside animal homes)
   Includes bibliographical references and index.
   Summary: "Full-color photographs and simple text describe beaver lodges"—Provided by publisher.
   ISBN 978-1-4296-6076-1 (library binding)
   1. Beavers—Habitations—Juvenile literature. I. Title.
QL737.R632P48 2012
599.37—dc22   2011000263

Editorial Credits
Katy Kudela, editor; Gene Bentdahl, designer; Marcie Spence, media researcher; Laura Manthe, production specialist

Photo Credits
Alamy: Arco Images GmbH, 13, Picture Press, 11; iStockphoto: jeffhochstrasser, 1, LucyF, 7, stanley45, 9;
Photolibrary/Peter Arnold, Inc: Laurent Piechegut, 15, Lynda Richardson, 21; Photo Researchers, Inc.:
Mark Newman, cover, Tom & Pat Leeson, 17; Photoshot Holdings: Jen & Des Bartlett, 5, Wolfgang Bayer, 19

Note to Parents and Teachers

The Look Inside Animal Homes series supports national science standards related to life
science. This book describes and illustrates beaver lodges. The images support early readers
in understanding the text. The repetition of words and phrases helps early readers learn new
words. This book also introduces early readers to subject-specific vocabulary words, which are
defined in the Glossary section. Early readers may need assistance to read some words and to
use the Table of Contents, Glossary, Read More, Internet Sites, and Index sections of the book.

Printed in the United States of America in North Mankato, Minnesota.
112011   006464R

Table of Contents

A Home for Beavers

Beavers live in lodges
all year long.
A family of four
to eight beavers lives
in one lodge.

Building a Beaver's Lodge

Beavers build lodges in lakes
or ponds. They sometimes build
dams on rivers or streams.
The dam makes a pond
of still, deep water.

Beavers build the lodge

in a few days.

They cut down many trees

with their sharp front teeth.

Beavers cut and pile

branches in the pond.

The lodge stands

up to 6 feet (1.8 meters)

above the water.

Beavers fill the spaces between

the branches with mud.

They leave one or two air holes

at the top of the lodge.

13

Inside a Beaver's Lodge

Underwater openings let beavers swim in and out of the lodge. Predators can't see beavers go in or out. Lodges keep beavers safe.

The lodge has one room.

Beavers sleep and eat

inside the lodge's dry room.

They bring in bark, twigs,

and leaves to eat.

A female beaver gives birth

inside the lodge.

Between two and four kits

are born each spring.

19

Kits live in the lodge

with their parents

for two years.

They then leave to

build their own homes.

Glossary

dam—a wall built across a stream or river that holds back water

kit—a young beaver

lodge—a beaver home; beavers eat, sleep, and raise their young in a lodge

predator—an animal that hunts other animals for food

still—not moving; quiet and calm

stream—a small river

twig—a small, thin branch of a tree or other woody plant

Read More

George, Lynn. *Beavers: Dam Builders*. Animal Architects. New York: PowerKids Press, 2011.

Green, Emily K. *Beavers*. Backyard Wildlife. Minneapolis: Bellwether Media, 2011.

Internet Sites

FactHound offers a safe, fun way to find Internet sites related to this book. All of the sites on FactHound have been researched by our staff.

Here's all you do:

Visit *www.facthound.com*

Type in this code: 9781429660761

Index

Word Count: 184

Grade: 1

Early-Intervention Level: 14